MAKE HIM LISTEN

KAREN KELLOCK PH.D.

Manual for
Superior Men

A complete theory based on Einstein physics,
Political Psychology, Systems Theory
and Archetypal Psychiatry.

FORMULA
All success attraction
All disease obstruction
All recovery elimination

You must fast on all three
OBSTRUCTIONS:
People
Habit
Food

MAKE HIM LISTEN

Systems theory: all mental illness is rooted in attachment trauma--we are *framed* by the SYSTEM. By framing us they either mess us up for life or we take that suit off and put a new on one, and go on. Because they're not awake living in their present moment they aren't working with a full deck and will bury the truth to death. Few are smart, the bulb's dim or out on most.

PEOPLE AND MIND
BLOCK SUCCESS

PEOPLE AND MIND
BLOCK SUCCESS

PEOPLE WERE THE PROBLEM

You're so high even your own associates or spouse come around too much & you gotta kick em out.

Don't feed the bears cuz they'll break into your house for it. Learn your lesson about people & quick.

You can't climb the mountain of success by holding on to weight of the past. You must clear a space.

You have to get rid of something--making room--for something new to come. That's how it is hon'.

For something new to come in something old must go and then you NEVER go back or fall below.

CHOSENS EXPERIENCE HATRED

I've experienced more hate than anyone I know. The way I grew up I'd never go back to my old home.

People today feel entitled to the goodies without doing the work--then they are jealous of achievers.

It's a pyrrhic victory: the scammer got 300 outa you but it boomeranged--now you're up/they're screwed.

They know what they did so when coming back they'll be a little stooped over/not so arrogant.

If the one in front of you can do it, you can do it too. That's the greatest thing to remember Sue.

FAULTY RELATIONS

As long as you stay around those people it will not get better, only worse. They waste your time sir.

RELOCATION IS OFTEN A MUST

You have to get away--FAR away--from those people. It's a spiritual thing, the time-wasters are evil.

They will suck you right back in. They want you right there to deal with the stuff they're peddlin'.

They want you right there, to pepper you with all their crazy tactics, antics and melodramatics.

In the process you can't say anything to defend yourself or object cuz they'll turn it around/blame you for it.

They make the wrong move and they panic. Instead of correcting course they run, ghost, ignore it.

Things got exposed and they know you know it. Instead of talking it out they fly away in a total panic.

As long as stuff keeps happening you've got your answer: they're never going to change sir.

ISOLATION THEN GOOD RELATIONS

Spiritually deep connections give you the emotional support necessary to face life's challenges see.

You need healing from deep wounds from prior experiences. These require attention and care sis.

Solitude is best for healing which requires time and introspection. It was awful but you're on the mend.

Confronting these open wounds is essential to build a bright future without being encumbered.

By healing these wounds you're making space for new opportunities and great people/positive energies.

Your ability to transform pain into personal growth makes you an inspiration to everyone you know.

By your transformation and very life you demonstrate it's possible to overcome adversity and thrive.

YOU ARE PREPARING FOR PURPOSE

You are being prepared for a great purpose and this requires periods of isolation from the chaos.

Isolation is needed to refine your skills and strengthen your resilience after overcoming the nuisance.

In solitude you receive revelations guilding you to purpose. Undistracted, you're now magnificence.

The depth of your soul intimidates any. You carry a wisdom few can reach and it's isolating see.

Your ability to see beyond appearances and feel energies make em feel exposed and fidgety.

Your depth is frightening cuz it requires them to face themselves without masks: they can't do that.

YOUR AUTHENTICITY IS A LIGHT

Your authenticity is a light and guide for others to follow but it will also repel those not ready to grow.

You're now a natural leader and source of inspiration. You must realize how valuable you are son.

True strength is the ability to face and overcome difficulties and you've had those in spades.

Your solitude is not a sign of weakness but a crucial phase in your growth journey. Revel in it, enjoy.

You are powerful, unique & destined for great things. Your solitude is a prelude to extraordinary living.

Keep shining cuz the world needs your light. So never feel ashamed that you want to be alone, aye!

FAMILY TRASHED YOUR IMAGE

They hurt you so much. They trashed your image/ruined your rep: that was family, the whole bunch.

Your heart was not created to be broken. You've wasted too much time and energy on the unawoken.

God gets tired of mending your broken heart cuz you trust the same useless/smiling upstarts.

You put love and trust in people who don't put love and trust in God Himself, creating your own hell.

Why are you alone and sad? Cuz those relationships didn't have God in em & you tolerated bad.

If God isn't in your relationships/marriage they are not going to work. You're lucky you escaped that jerk.

WALKING AWAY GENTLY

The best decision you have ever made was walking away. Now you'll succeed & really make hay.

Tho' you be sad and lonely, you're getting your STRENGTH back and you will continue to: fact.

As you get your PEACE back you'll get your JOY back and that's a promise from God, your dad.

You'll be damned to let anyone in your life who'll take any/everything again, that life is over friend.

You're a GREAT: unencumbered by other people & what they think—about you or anything else see.

DUMPER'S REMORSE

If you were discarded, know the narcissist suffers from dumper's remorse, suicide thoughts or worse.

Dumper's remorse doesn't come from guilt but from losing a source of supply too early, aye.

They lost admiration & support they received from you, not knowing at the time they'd be screwed.

Don't beg em back: the more you distance yourself the more they face the consequences [sad sack].

With time their pain sets in: not from remorse for pain they caused you but from being alone again.

A narc does consider the consequences of actions but their perspective remains self-centered son.

They think about what they've lost--the SUPPLY you provided--and reality hits hard, tho' one-sided.

THE BRUTAL SMEAR CAMPAIGN

They question their brutal smear campaign--marking the narc--and wonder if they were too extreme.

But the real jolt comes entering a new relationship and not being fulfilled and supplied as you did.

By the time the narc wakes up & wants you back you're on your own journey and say "no way Mack."

Your changed attitude does not go unnoticed by the narcissist. He feels unsettled & you are missed.

When the narc attempts to hoover you back in, he's not straightforward but makes little hints.

The narc prefers to wait for you to open up to him again, avoiding any vulnerability on his part friend.

Since he ended the relationship he's reluctant to come down from his position of power or to suffer.

HE WANTS YOU TO CHASE HIM

He wants you to chase after him but you won't my friend so he's stuck in dumper's remorse again.

They long for the connection you once had but too proud to admit mistakes or grovel for your hand.

You've gotta be willing to walk away. If you stay when not valued, you tell Self it's all you deserve ok.

If they take you for granted you'll be drained. That's if you let them--and it will increase every day.

They'll take and take without a thought of your needs or giving back. That's just the way it is: fact.

If you're the type to keep giving, to keep pouring yourself out, you'll have nothing left: ouch.

THE DIFFICULTY SETTING BOUNDARIES

The answers are to leave or set boundaries. But they're not used to you standing up for self see.

Some are only in your life cuza what they get from you. It's not YOU, you must discern between the two.

You're just a resource: something they can tap into whenever it's convenient for them of course.

If you don't draw that line they'll continue to take whatever the need: food, sex or money see.

USERS NEVER CONSIDER THE COST

Takers & users never think about the cost to you. That's never an issue and the results can be cruel.

Careless: They're so focused on what they're getting they never stop to consider what you're losing.

Continue pouring into people who don't give back and you'll run on empty, bringing more abuse see.

When you hit empty they won't be there to refill, moving on to the next person with better supply still.

This same user will call you selfish for setting boundaries. In a rotten world this is common see.

You've reached this point: no matter how much they try to deceive you get closer to your true self see.

When people come in with deceptive intentions God always sees it. You may not but will evade it.

You will trust God more and more to protect and vindicate you even when you're blind too.

VINDICATION IS THE LORD'S

You stop trying to get back at scum for you know your God will always do it better tho' you're dumb.

God protected me even when in sin for He knew who I'd be and saw me that way anyway friend.

Become shrewd: see through people but don't let em know you know. Stay on top of your frenemy foe.

It starts with dressing nice/caring what you look like. Then it's your home then seeing details: yikes!

You notice things about people and become hypercritical. You begin to understand/discern evil.

Don't think of the past when you put up with ghastly, gross things from your guests and other pests.

Become a teacher and understand the little children so desperate for moral and cleanliness educatin'.

LIBERALISM DEGRADED HABITS

Since WWII liberal thought took over. It was the sex revolution that degraded us more than ever.

People became lax, lazy, not-quite-clean, shady. They let things slip, they did not enforce a tight ship.

Imagine a woman knowing her dog isn't housebroken bringing him into your home. Doggone!

We let things slide, tolerating too much. This happens inch by inch 'til the whole culture is dirty as such.

Those who put their foot down seen as bitchy harridans who could even bring violence in on them.

Putting foot down wakes people up. Esp. after three generations of this stuff, even seniors are stuck.

If you're a tidy person you're imposed on just by them walking in. You're not momma/can't educate em.

You meet someone new and have to educated em on how to treat you. The considerate are very few.

Like personal grooming in front of you, or picking their teeth after stew: it's all disgusting to you.

We've become a buncha hillbillies since the classy forties when appearance was everything see.

BEING CHOSEN AND UNNOTICED

As a chosen you're prepared most when feeling lost and abandoned: a test when nothing's happenin'.

You've repented of sins and still you're sitting there with nothing happening. This is part of the test/plan.

When viewing them you sense superfluity when you're happy in your simplicity. It's a separation see.

God has a purpose for you and you're ready for it but still you wait: this is where you show faith.

You've separated but still you're bound. This is where you put up with em in silence but aplomb.

Your path as a chosen is designed by God so it's not up to people to understand or validate at all.

Not getting approval or fame is just another test while you wait. Being unnoticed is hard to take.

HOW TO TAKE NOTHINGNESS

As you give up on the outer you go inward, believing the divine will support you. Now you benefit Sue.

Seeing how every obstacle was part of that purpose is part of the trip. Vacuity--nothingness--is a tip.

Go with the nothingness, welcome it. With the divine no one else sees have a regal relationship.

God has control of everything under heaven. To the stultifying silence and nothingness, welcome.

You have a natural majesty but can't show it yet. They know nothing about it so just wait for it.

Let nothingness strengthen not break you. It will hone your spirit and intuition if you can take it Sue.

Solitude has polished your character and you've risen strong and more determined than the others.

If you can forget the awful past [never going there] God will substitute with prosperity and happiness.

HARD OBSTACLES WERE PART OF THE PLAN

Those hard obstacles were not signs of failure but opportunities to gro--so now you know.

Even being scammed with money, God will replace it all honey. For what better lesson can there be see?

You were picked for your resilience. You have the fortitude to persevere after years of tears.

After all that your have the discernment to guide and finally take the lead. It took all of that see.

As you approach the beginning of your next chapter the cosmos now works in your favor: it's all there.

The good things make you feel better about yourself but are evidence of your persistence thru hell.

ERA OF NOTHINGNESS

Knowing these great things that are soon coming make your era of nothingness less numbing.

Just get thru it tho' it's hard to take. The ego wants approval cus we're human: it's that we gotta break.

Your final triumph will speak for itself and those who questioned you will be silenced, so what.

Now those forces against you work towards your highest advantage and wealth you can manage.

It's written in the stars you will ascend: it is INEVITABLE. So forget apprehensions, relax now.

All along the cosmos has prepared you for this very moment. Thru the crap or nothingness, you know it.

Your gifts are a direct outcome of your faith and work. When your time has come you'll come first.

FAITH WHEN NOTHING'S HAPPENING

You have a steadfast conviction in your mission. Even in the fog of strife and hopeless livin' you held on.

You must prosper to set an example for others. To encourage when nothing's happening there.

Things formerly seen as thorny barriers now become the cornerstone of your success: believe this.

Being chosen is a supernatural mission setting you apart in ways they can't see/are suspicious of see.

You weren't picked by accident but for meaning and purpose. Never give up on this, it's coming sis.

You possess a potent quality that can't be duplicated or copied and that sets you apart, often lonely.

You've pushed past obstacles and accomplished tasks others find impossible or unthinkable, alas!

Difficulties, hardships and intensely lonely periods are paths of the chosen and it's all for a reason.

These difficulties are intended to mold you into the tough, robust bearing you were born to show.

Maintaining composure in the face of overwhelming odds: these are the ones called upon by God.

Those who are not up to the task are not called & just part of the mob tho' they still face God's rod.

Knowing these things about yourself, you gird yourself up to do your work after overcoming hell.

TOLERATING NOTHINGNESS

Chosen: how you tolerate the era of nothingness is a mark of your strength, endurance and progress!

Your kindness to the wee ones stuck in mindless superfluity is a mark of your humility & generosity!

For you KNOW your time is coming: that too is a mark of faith. You look stunning and lost weight!

Realizing no one cares about you can change your life. It's scary at first but then you go to God, aye.

You were chosen cuz you passed the test other's couldn't: you maintained calm with problems.

This test wasn't mental/physical but spiritual, measuring the vitality of your soul that's all.

That bright light shining within you directed every action and THAT'S why you were divinely chosen.

When everything around seemed entirely hopeless and overpowering you just kept on shining.

And thus when things got so bad they suddenly changed into good: the test was understood.

God let you go through setbacks and betrayals cuz they built strength and character for you all.

These are all lessons learned, not losses. The chosen have no losses no matter what the gossip.

IGNORE THE MIND'S ILLUSIONS

Ignore the mind's illusions. See it as noise or distant people talking not YOU, the true self son.

You are not your mind for the mind is a thief: it wants to take you back or fear the future not just BE.

The mind is just a tool but it captures us in it's web. It's the true self behind that's as peaceful as it gets.

When the mind takes you back or forward you must control it. Seek only the peace without it.

The uncontrolled mind agitates, strikes fear & triggers anger. Let it go and work hard on this, or suffer.

The vast nothingness behind the busy mind is the True Self and it's also in happy unity with the ALL.

SEEK NOTHINGNESS BEHIND MIND

Being part of the ALL does not mean you're undistinguished: it could be your needed genius.

The busy mind is ego driven and tends towards angry separation: that's not the True Self son.

The vast nothingness of peace is how you were as a child, just acting not thinking everything out.

Just BE and let the mind go. It's just a tool to get things done not the YOU we all wanna get to know.

POLITHOUGHT

How to destroy a country: open borders, take guns, kill the babies, raise taxes & support your enemies.

BEYOND BACKSTABBERS

BEYOND BACKSTABBERS

AFTER BEING SCAMMED

Being shocked, scammed, disrupted, betrayed or robbed can reveal the true self. It's a paradox.

Let's say you're scammed for $300. The hurt takes down the illusions hiding your inner core son.

Just block the person then start over again. Shut it all out then look for the miracle inside, amen.

As much as it hurts, shut it out--by realizing your inner core will now come forth, beautiful & devout.

It's the REALIZATION of the process that allows you to deal with the scam or rejection, isn't that nice?

You've blocked the charlatan knowing God'll get em. Now wait for the miracle inside, and THANK em!

LET IT TRIGGER AN INNER MIRACLE

It took this scam/rejection to TRIGGER the inner miracle of the true self coming out after a debacle.

So you trusted again and was betrayed again. Obviously you needed this lesson so thank em.

You'll be scammed until you learn your lesson. Thank the scammer for the last one as you're risin'.

Remember, for the true self to awake it TOOK this giant shake so revel in that, not the guy on the take.

Being scammed makes you trust your loved ones more. That's another benefit you should thank em for.

BEYOND BACKSTABBERS

$300 is a small price to pay for the emergence of the True Self and being stronger than you were ok.

Events like being scammed can do you a world of good if the process of transformation is understood.

It's a funny thing but as we get stronger we trust humans less not more. Now you will soar.

Trust and love your inner circle but even they're on probation if you wanna be totally certain.

KNOWING THE PROCESS IS SUCCESS

Knowing the process of the True Self reborn, I was totally elated when scammed to the core.

God'll get em, you know He will. So forget em and focus on your unique diamond emerging from hell.

Being scammed can kick the life outa you. Your self-esteem can plunge but not with this new view.

Look what you're getting after the disaster. It's your profitable true self coming out by this trigger.

After the scam a whole new world opened up to me. I was elated, felt so cosmic and entirely free.

You trusted again and the minute you paid em they were gone. Another lesson learned from the throng.

It didn't make sense such joy after being taken for 300 but I was ELATED cuz the self was a thunder.

TRY THIS EXERCISE WHEN SCAMMED

Try this exercise when scammed: forget it now wait for the miracle. Got it? WAIT for the miracle man.

BEYOND BACKSTABBERS

When scammed you gotta sink or swim and that's enough to trigger the true self's emergin'.

The best part is you're done with the scammer. It's a done deal now, no more questions or wonder.

That alone is enough to start a new cycle of prosperity. Create a SPACE for the new adventure see.

Just as good is the fact you must trust God. He WILL VINDICATE, it's a promise for you to hang on.

SATAN LOVES YOU BEING SCAMMED

Satan loves the scam cuz people give up. That's when you gotta push ahead anyway and LOOK UP.

Congratulations! For the low price of $300 you got your True Self back and can now prosper w/out lack.

Once you've eaten crow & blocked the scammer watch the boomerang occur as God vindicates for sure.

Substitute thoughts immediately. Don't waste any more time on the charlatan who stole your money.

Instead of resenting the scammer, substitute thoughts w/what you got: your true self from the disaster.

You've gotta God who protects His sons & daughters. Don't give it another thought & forget the scammer.

You can't go thru something like that and not get something out of it. WAIT for God to settle it.

ADVERSITY STRENGTHENS YOU

Any adversity that doesn't kill you will only strengthen you. You're about to witness a miracle, whew!

BEYOND BACKSTABBERS

You think your loving God won't vindicate this? He will and fast, don't resent the scam another minute.

When things like scams happen, KNOW God will vindicate and get right back to work mate.

HOW TO DISCERN SCAMMERS

It takes painful lessons to achieve a SHARP EYE. To unravel the "good intentions" of others, aye.

We must learn the signs of empty promises. In a fake world it's essential, and you didn't know this.

When you learn to decode human enigmas you can enter the path of genuine human relationships.

Your hyper-awareness after being scammed is the first step towards change: to discern the deranged.

Empty promises: they disappear like a puff of smoke. Sudden silence, no delivery, they're a ghost.

They were all performance, a tool & manipulation to get what they wanted when you were unguarded.

In these relationships they vanish when you need em the most. That's a pattern with these folks.

They never really backed you, only what they could extract from you. It's obvious to the shrewd.

THEY LEAVE YOU IN THE LURCH

For those left in the lurch the pain of betrayal is a valuable lesson. Now YOU'RE the shrewd one.

Recognizing this behavior is crucial in discerning those seeking to use you. Empty promises are cruel.

BEYOND BACKSTABBERS

Their actions speak volumes about intentions. Disdainful comments erode confidence man.

One diminutive comment at a time: those who use others for personal gain are experts at this, aye.

These comments are subtle or passed off as humor. They chip away at your self-esteem by the hour.

Such harmless banter has sharp edges. The AIM is to pull you down not lift you up: these are the methods.

THEY DOWNPLAY YOUR ACHIEVEMENTS

They laugh at your successes and downplay your achievements: just one word does it sis.

It's psychological warfare: by undervaluing your accomplishments they create unbalance quick.

The more self-doubt you have the easier to manipulate. Your insecurity means they can dominate.

Belittling you gives them a false sense of superiority and they need that to cover their own insecurity.

It's vital to recognize this behavior, to see beyond the superficial charm and discern the scammer.

Once you recognize the toxic dynamic you have two choices: distance yourself or be ok with it.

WHAT ARE YOU GETTING OUT OF IT?

Unilateral benefit: they benefit from the relationship but you don't. What you get is zero, a joke.

They constantly ask for favors but are absent when you need help. That's a dead giveaway, that's all.

BEYOND BACKSTABBERS

One benefits at the expense of the other. If it's sex, the other is degraded morally in self-disgust sir.

The user draws nourishment emotional/financial w/out contributing to the host, becoming a ghost.

The root is self-centeredness and lack of empathy. Everything is about them, it's narcissism see.

IDENTIFY THIS PATTERN!

Identify this pattern by the lack of reciprocity. You feeling shortchanged should be enough see.

They disregard your needs or feelings. It's all about their desires while yours they're neglecting.

You get no support when vulnerable. It's not inconsiderate but calculated, to maintain control.

They must constantly keep you unbalanced to degrade your worth. Recognize emotional neglect first.

Emotional manipulators are masters of disguise. Caring at first, soon their true colors come through, aye.

They play with your emotions inducing anxiety. They lift you way up only to then cut you down see.

You're like a plant tended by a careless gardener: left to die from neglect or sometimes overwatered.

BACK AND FORTH DESTABILIZES

Going back and forth destabilizes the system where you will constantly seek their approval friend.

You'll do anything to regain the warmth and affection they once gave you. This makes you a fool.

BEYOND BACKSTABBERS

In this dynamic they hold all the power. They're king or queen of the hour and it's you they devour.

They decide when to show affection and when to withdraw it. You're desperate, pulling your hair out.

It's all about one thing: controlling you while you depend on them emotionally in a mind screw.

SCAM INTERACTIONS TANK SELF-ESTEEM

You need to understand how these interactions affect your self-esteem and emotional well being.

Support: Emotional investment doled out only by what they stand to gain. Otherwise it's indifference ok.

Recognizing the lack of support is vital to see the reality of this person. There's no reciprocity here man.

Every act is a competition: every move they make is not to advance you but undermine you son.

It's not about you growing together but outdoing, outshining and proving themselves to be superior.

The root of their behavior is insecurity. Hope this helps to know this, though it sure hurts if needy.

Their self-worth is not tied to accomplishment but ability to outshine others: what a bummer!

FOR THEM TO WIN YOU LOSE

In their mind, for them to win you have to lose. It's always gonna be that way with the cruel.

This zero sum mentality turns all interactions into a battle for dominance and YOU end as dunce.

BEYOND BACKSTABBERS

It's exhausting: instead of collaboration everything's met with rivalry. Recognize this and get free!

Instead of celebrating your successes they see them as threats. Just when you win they get pissed.

Instead of supporting you with challenges, they exploit them instead. Try to get this through your head.

IDENTIFY PETTY COMPETITORS

Identifying petty competitors is essential for peace of mind. I've especially seen it with womenkind.

After they scam you and disappear, if you get em under your. control again NEVER FORGET sir.

You made a mint so they're back again, real friendly. Don't forget how they were when needy.

It's good when you're in control again, being rich. But never forget how they were when in a ditch.

Oh, they're so syrupy nice again aren't they. You're such a nice guy/lady you wanna forget the shady.

Don't take em back or you'll lose control again. You gotta stay on top for you are the chosen.

Chosens GOTTA stay on top or it's a severe drop when the phonies are in control and you're a flop.

Tell em you're rich again even if you aren't. Do anything to get em back so you can be the star.

They'll always be there when you're in the sun but when dark clouds arise they'll pick up & be gone.

WHY CHOSENS ARE ALONE

BEYOND BACKSTABBERS

Your authenticity repels those who are not sincere. Your light makes those with masks feel weird.

Being authentic means living without filters. Showing the self, virtues and vulnerabilities out there.

Your honesty is unsettling to those unaccustomed to transparency. But it'll make you famous see.

Your presence forces them to face their shadows. They'd rather avoid then do that ya know.

YOUR TRANSPARENCY ISOLATES

Your clear transparency isolates you but also purifies your environment of bad influences too.

You're in-your-face authenticity attracts only the genuine and that's a profitable thing see.

Surrounded by people appreciating your truth, you can now build relationships based on trust, whew!

Your ability to maintain authenticity deepens character and strengthens connections in the future.

Your vibrational energy is too high for many. Every being perceives vibrations/frequency and you're a heavy.

Those who can't keep up feel intimidated/distance themselves. It's natural as the universe separates out.

YOUR HIGH VIBRATIONS ATTRACT/REPEL

Your high vibrations attract and repel at the same time. It's a sign of your great power & charisma, aye.

Only those elevating themselves to your level can stay by your side. Hold on to them for dear life!

BEYOND BACKSTABBERS

Isolation creates a space where only those who truly resonate can enter. This relieves you greatly.

Being surrounded with such high frequency satellites means you can all grow together, unbothered.

This natural selection and holy separation means you only experience harmonious interactions.

Your inborn high frequency likely made your early days miserable, as you weren't understood at all.

Now you'll attract opportunities that MATCH your energetic vibration, as like attracts like son.

THE LAW OF AFFINITY

It's the LAW OF AFFINITY: like attracting like. This affinitization of atoms will be your success, aye.

You had to eliminate the clutter--the scammers--to rise to this level of success and to finally prosper.

Your inner peace will now be your first priority. Your serenity is fundamental to maintaining it all see.

When you refuse to allow anyone in who disturbs your harmony, you become very selective see.

Inner peace is a precious gift. I'm sure you finally realize this now that you're rid of that recent grift.

GUARD YOUR INNER PEACE FIRST

Your inner peace requires care & protection. This inner attitude may seem selfish but it's survival son.

Being selective means you're creating a safe space where your soul can thrive without interference ok.

BEYOND BACKSTABBERS

With calm mind and serene heart you'll make perfect decisions and create a new world revolution.

Will your isolation mean success? YES! By the great law of affinitization as I previously expressed.

You will now attract people and situations that respect your need for tranquility. It'll be a real party.

Your ability to maintain serenity makes you a beacon of stability, a valuable asset to the world see.

SEEK AUTHENTIC CONNECTIONS

You seek authentic connections & meaningful relationships now. That means a success team, wow!

This all leads you to avoid superficial connections. You'd rather be alone than social like them.

Your isolation is a sign of strength not weakness. To them being always alone is a hideous image.

Superficial connections offer companionship without satisfying your need for real authenticity see.

You need **DEPTH** in relationships. This characterizes your keen spirit tho' others can't understand it.

SELF-WORTH TAKES A LIFETIME

IF THINGS AREN'T WORKING
THINGS HAPPEN & IT'S OVER
TURNING REJECTION INTO ADVANTAGE
NEVER PRESSURE RESPONSE
SHOW YOUR VALUE THRU WISDOM
YOUR DISAPPEARANCE
CUT OFF ALL CONTACT
ACT AS IF HE DOESN'T EXIST
SELF-WORTH TOOK A LIFETIME
NOT TAUGHT SELF-LOVE
LATE LIFE REALIZATIONS
THEY HATE WITHOUT CAUSE
IT'S CLASSY NOT TO WORRY
YOU'RE DIFFERENT FROM THEM
RELEASE THE HATERS
SCREWED UP FAMILIES
YOU WON'T THINK OF THEM LATER

SELF-WORTH TAKES
A LIFETIME

IF THINGS AREN'T WORKING

If things aren't working you can't make them work. You just gotta drop off or cut it off for sure.

Often times it's just God's timing. Nothing lasts forever an there's been an irreparable parting.

He won't listen cuz people are selfish. They're into their own thing and have their own purposes.

If you're a chosen you just buck up and bite your way thru it. Joy comes in the morning, bet on it.

People get sick, old, bored or just annoyed. You can't count on constant love, it's time to avoid.

You can't make someone listen, it's asking a legless man to run a race. Either accept things or go ok.

THINGS HAPPEN & IT'S OVER

Fortuitous events happen and suddenly the relationship is over. This is life, even for the most clever.

His feelings click off like a switch, yours follow to self-protect and a downward spiral hits the decks.

If older a heart attack could happen or you now need oxygen: relationship problems are sudden.

SELF WORTH TAKES A LIFETIME

When secure you thought you were strong but now in anxiety it seems you will never get along.

My advice here is to avoid, not fight. Sparks of fire will not help this matter, just get back your light.

If older your heart may flutter and this can be dangerous as this is serious and nothing cuts deeper.

You always fought it out before as to who's wrong or right. I'd advise to get past this and go light.

You gotta take care of yourself now, it's a mushroom cloud that's dangerous to health you know.

Think it through and stay calm. Not like most of the world taking a beer right now or calling mom.

You'll be ok, turn on a prayer channel today. Take control though I know it hurts like hell ok.

TURNING REJECTION INTO ADVANTAGE

When someone ignores you, ignore them too. Turn this event into an opportunity for growth Sue.

See situations as not just things to endure but a chance to grow with patience and wisdom sir.

Instead of reflecting their indifference, embark on a journey of self-discovery & your interests.

Focus on your own values and embrace emotional independence then it hurts far less.

It's not about winning a trivial attention game but mastering the art of inner peace ok.

Be your own playwright: write your story with dignity and sincerity and this gives control quickly.

SELF WORTH TAKES A LIFETIME

I had to control emotions to stop a racing heart. In our latter days our health is the biggest part.

I know it's hard to say but don't react emotionally. I was emotionally ill for days but not displayed.

It's difficult to not react when ignored but the best reaction is to stay calm any way you can.

Can you internally reflect not emotionally react? That's our goal in this dyad, go within God said.

Tranquility is essential but understanding is crucial: seeing this prickly system in a nutshell.

Responding with dignity & respect means being friendly and polite. Can you do that despite?

NEVER PRESSURE RESPONSE

Never pressure response from a need for validation. Keep that crap outa this, it's gone beyond.

If he ignores you still, avoid confrontation or signs of weakness. You're a playwright remember sis?

Controlling actions shows strength and self-confidence. No more demanding miss.

Recognize other's behavior shouldn't alter your self-image or values. Hold your head high Sue.

Focus on things under your control and ignore those that aren't, that's where you should start.

If he ignores you, REMOVE HIM from your mind. Don't think of him or you're back in the grind.

Start by shifting all focus on him to yourself. When he comes to mind say "NO!": hope this helps.

SELF WORTH TAKES A LIFETIME

Make a list of your goals and work actively to achieve them. This puts all focus on yourself, amen?

Find a new hobby or start a new project. Make plans with family & friends and don't look back.

Enjoy time with others and leave time to reflect on self. This is not selfishness, it's the only help.

Continual improvement will create a positive mindset. More and more the rejecter seems all wet.

Soon you'll realize their indifference doesn't matter. It'll be laughable if you continue this way sir.

Facing situations in which you're ignored is a chance to demonstrate your value backed by the Lord.

SHOW YOUR VALUE THRU WISDOM

Show your value thru wisdom, kindness and integrity. Remember fighting this the opposite way?

Engage respectfully by humbly sharing your knowledge as if you're a third party in this marriage.

Listen attentively instead of seeking response or validation. Be like a nice neighbor son.

Forget him and be true to yourself by demonstrating strength and stoic values facing this hell.

Self-improvement with respect for others shows your stuff every time. Let this be your guiding line.

By showing you remain balanced and respectful regardless of them is attractive tho' bold.

YOUR DISAPPEARANCE

SELF WORTH TAKES A LIFETIME

When you disappear out of their lives it does not end well. It's even worse when you're respectful.

When a chosen one leaves lives it blunts their potential and leaves them feeling empty in a nutshell.

You helped & nurtured them. You continuously brought good suggestions and now that's gone son.

When you disappear everything falls apart but if you're begging and whining they'll only depart.

When you show up things are more complete. Without you in the picture they're lost, unsweet.

They thought they're doing the right thing but behold: everything comes crumbling down/no gold.

Just as a breakup brings on emotional illness, you gotta control those emotions of wreck this.

CUT OFF ALL CONTACT

If love's grown cold the best thing you can do is cut off contact: cease communication or have less.

Don't send messages & cease responding to texts. Do this or emotional illness becomes a hex.

Mental illness won't affect the body the way the emotional will. I can feel the pain still.

When love has grown cold—with someone you were so close to—it's like a heart amputation Sue.

If he doesn't respond stop contacting him at all. Silence is golden when dealing with old beaus.

Especially with women, the emotional level is strong, laid bare, intense and liable to a terrible end.

SELF WORTH TAKES A LIFETIME

Women must protect their emotions and that means **NO CONTACT** whether in person or phone.

What if you're living with him? Same thing: keep it to a minimum and the essential only, amen.

Most importantly, avoid eye contact. That's no small thing since it used to send you to heaven, fact.

Start doing things you enjoy. Get out more: take a walk, meet a friend, lay in the sun and feel the joy.

Maintaining a positive mood will remind you of your value. You were rejected--it was him not you.

Self-improvement is always the right response to being ignored. Your self-esteem was hurt/lowered.

Exercising, hobbies and learning new skills are excellent elevators of your battered self-worth, killed.

Cultivate character and contribute to home or society. You're a rare one with much to give sweetie.

ACT AS IF HE DOESN'T EXIST

If one ignores you, acting as they don't exist is the right response. They started it: you're not a dunce.

It's easier to move on than fix a situation over which you have no control. They started it you know.

Use the silent treatment as a form of self reflection and emotional regulation. It's the only way son.

During the silent treatment, reflect on your thoughts and feelings. Come within, that's all there is.

Ignore the outer, concentrate on the inner. Love your pets: they are our precious therapies forever.

SELF WORTH TAKES A LIFETIME

Silence is not selfish, it promotes a sense of inner peace and self-control for its main purposes.

Silence avoids behaviors seen as manipulative or vengeful of which we've had a mouthful.

The minute you first feel sad it's a red flag. You've tolerated so long so make plans to be gone.

When ignored, don't beg for attention. Instead, make em know they're losing something son.

Instead of vying for attention, find satisfaction in your own achievements. For the ignored, this is best.

When ignored, be kind but emotionally distant. This is most aristocratic and it cracks the whip.

After all that, it doesn't matter any more. Toxic people are irrelevant for God has shifted the score.

They were there to make you tough. Bold certainty is written on your face but your kind not rough.

SELF-WORTH TOOK A LIFETIME

t took you a lifetime to know your worth. Not knowing it caused people/men to abuse you girl.

Low self-esteem triggered constant mistreatment, it was like a drill instructor in a regiment.

You were hit & hit til you woke up to your own spirit. This built social muscle, you had to go thru it.

You were no longer their punching bag or abuse puppet, knowing you were more worthy then that.

This is making gold, preceding by FIRE to burn out the dross. It had to be so thank God and go forth.

SELF WORTH TAKES A LIFETIME

Now you're rare cuz you know who you are. Most are part of a herd, moving together or in pairs.

NOT TAUGHT SELF-LOVE

You weren't taught your worth at a young age but the dysfunctional home produced a sage.

You may have seen bickering at home then at school made fun of: what misery you came out of!

You don't need smoke, drink, drugs or other things. You need your own spirit which goes away see.

My trauma is healed. If a young man wants my money I tell him to go to a bank, I don't need heels.

I don't like crowds, I love country. You can have your cruises I like old barns, cows and horses see.

LATE LIFE REALIZATIONS

These things I realized later in life. Solitude in nature is precious after social hypnotism and strife.

What I learned when old: I don't want mink stoles, I love some ol' vest I got at a thrift store long ago.

How could I go on a cruise, leaving my dogs & cats? That would be preposterous, I'd never do that.

I'd be seasick and claustrophobic on a cruise. I want the pleasures & comforts of home, you too?

Even just going to the store or mailbox I can't wait to go home. Pleasures & comfort, never to roam!

They thought you'd never make it outa your rut and their traps. But you did and they're axed.

SELF WORTH TAKES A LIFETIME

You don't have time for any more haters especially from your past, now get going daughter at last.

THEY HATE WITHOUT CAUSE

They're still gonna hate without cause, for you're pure of sin and fresh faced from your repentance.

For a creative discoverer, it's most important the work is done right regardless of how many they buy.

You're pretty, you're handsome. You've repented and purified so much you look like a statue son.

Let haters come at you, you're radiant cuz you've repented & God is finally showing through.

You're happy and well. There's no more sin/disease destroying your looks straight outa hell.

There's a spring in your step now, you've reached a new pinnacle and persecutors see your style.

IT'S CLASSY NOT TO WORRY

It's classy not to worry about haters. They don't have anything on you cuz you're a God lover.

The haters of your soul are baffled. They cannot believe you got so good after all that hassle.

After they humiliated your name and mocked your shooting for fame, you're now ok?

That makes you so much more starry in their eyes, the fact you could overcome all that, aye.

After they slandered you to everybody who would listen and wrote it in the papers, you're a winner?

SELF WORTH TAKES A LIFETIME

See the split: you continue getting better while they get worse til they die in the gutter/need a hearse.

For God doesn't take it lightly they hated His own. When pure He finally removes your groans.

YOU'RE DIFFERENT FROM THEM

You're now two different sides of the spectrum. When your war is resolved you've nothing in common.

You've got positive light, they negative darkness. You're never gonna fit now you have God's likeness.

But they'll watch you thru social media, you can be sure of that. They won't ever admit this, so what.

Keep prospering & getting better, given them even more reason to hate you: get used to it brother.

RELEASE THE HATERS

You gotta release those haters & do something better in life but worry about them in needless strife.

Keep smiling & be happy God woke you up: to who you really are, written in the stars, not good luck.

It took you so long to know your worth and it triggered constant mistreatment, remember it sir?

You weren't taught your worth at a young age. Coming from an abusive situation you felt not-OK.

When your own parents didn't instruct self-love it was something you had to learn from above.

You had to be slandered and smacked in the face to learn self-love: it was self-protect or rust.

SCREWED UP FAMILIES

SELF WORTH TAKES A LIFETIME

You may have seen mom opt in & out of relationships and the disrespect she tolerated from it.

You may have seen dad in and out of relationships. In & out, in & out: there was no stability kids.

How could you feel self worth, with no stability in parents showing love for each other girl?

Some were raised in two parent homes that were toxic. With such bickering how could you make it?

This destroyed the map in your template. It showed: at school you were made fun of & mocked ok.

Since you didn't know your worth they treated you bad. They'd test how far they could go with that.

I know cuz they did it to me too. In fact it lasted from kindergarten to graduate school, so cruel.

Now you know your worth from all the experiences you had will ill-hearted people: the irony of evil.

YOU WON'T THINK OF THEM LATER

Don't think when you're rich & famous you're gonna roll this over in mind, worrying about those kind.

No, this will all be gone starting today. Just the lessons learned will remain, the pain will dissolve ok.

Their ill-heartedness caused you to learn self-love and worth. You had to be burnt to learn it sir.

You finally learned after the last mistreatment that from birth on, you never knew it/parents blew it.

When it was finally the last straw you cut em off. That was your real birthday, the joyous blastoff.

SELF WORTH TAKES A LIFETIME

Ever notice how God removed em for you? They died, they moved away or seem to have vaporized.

Now they're confused, some have left the room or they just hate life with failing businesses too.

Some will always be disgusted with you but who cares, you've flown the coup & they are screwed.

You changed your number & don't wanna ever see them again. But that's what they get, amen.

They get what they dished but it wasn't just you. It was from your Father who evens things too.

MAKE HIM LISTEN

WE GO OUT ALONE
SELF-RELIANCE IS A MUST
WOMEN BOND DEEPER/QUICKER
MEMORY IS THE EVIL GLUE
BROKEN HEART = FRAGMENTED MEMORY
MEMORY AND BONDAGE
A BROKEN HEART GETS CROOKED
APOLOGIZE FOR ALL THE LIES
"I'M SO STUPID, I'M SO STUPID"
SICKLY CYCLICITY
WHY DO THEY PERSIST WITH THE NARCISSIST?
TRAUMA BONDS EXPLAIN IT ALL
SCARED AND SLANDERED SPEECHLESS
FLYING MONKEYS IN ASSIST
FLYING MONKEYS ARE CODEPENDENT
SCAPEGOATS ARE EXPOSED TARGETS
EXTREME MANIPULATION: SECRETS
TOP HANKERING OVER PEOPLE
HERO'S PATH LOOKS LIKE INSANITY
JEZEBELS GET THEIR HIT MEN AGAINST YOU
IN CLARITY THE PAST IS SCARY
EXHAUSTED BY IRRELEVANCE
SHORT ATTENTION SPAN
EGO BUCKET FULL OF HOLES
MY GENERATION HAD WORK HABITS
DYSFUNCTION MAKES US HOMESICK: IRONY
DID THE CHURCH HELP?
WHAT IS ATTACHMENT INJURY?
SHAME IS THE RESULT OF DISCONNECTION
EXISTENTIAL PANIC
THE MORE INTRICATE THE PATTERNS
ESCAPE INTO THE RIGHT BRAIN
AT HOME I'M FREE
LIMBIC RESONANCE OR IT'S HELL MAN

MAKE HIM LISTEN

LIBERAL SISTERS CAME BACK TO ABUSE US
ONCE IN SAFETY EXPECT PTSD
ATTACHMENT TRAUMA: BEING IGNORED
INTRUSIVE THINKING STARTS WITH BETRAYAL
PRESENT LONGING MIRRORS THE BEGINNING
BETRAYAL IS ATTACHMENT INJURY
RELEASING VICTIMHOOD FOR SUCCESS
NORMALIZE IT TO DISTANCE IT
MOVED TO A GHOST TOWN TO BE RID OF EM
ATTACHMENT INJURY = TRAUMA ENERGY
MAPS THE BRAIN AND IMPACTS NERVOUS SYSTEM
FORGET SPECIFICS AND SEE THE FOREST
EMOTIONAL BLOCK
STORED AT LEVEL OF ACTIVATION
FACE THE EARLY CREEPS OR DENY AND REPEAT
THE FLIP FLOP OF STORED ENERGY
USE PRESENT GRIEF TO ERASE TEMPLATE
SO YOUR EX HAS NEW SUPPLY
DEVALUATION PHASE: NOW HE COMES OUT
MOVE ON AHEAD NOW—LET DEAD BURY DEAD
THEY'RE JUST DOING THEIR THING/RUNNING THEIR NUMBER
JEALOUSY FOR CLOSENESS OR DISTANCE
SUDDEN LOVE LOSS: SURVIVAL MODE
HE DEVALUED AND DISCARDED YOU
THEY CAN TURN ON THE CHARM
SELF-LOVE STAVES OFF ABUSE
NEVER ALLOW CASUAL EX-SEX
DON'T BE A DAM FOOL
AGEISM
FOOD MEANS MOTHER AND AGE SHOULDN'T MATTER
GOVERNMENT THOUGHTS
FATARIAN THOUGHTS BACK THEN
COMPLETION INTO SUCCESS AT LAST
LEFT WING INSTITUTIONS ARE COLLAPSING
THINKERS NEED TWO HOUSES
KK BOOKS: BEING DIFFERENT IS DANGEROUS

BRIEF OBSTACLES

I lived in the dark and attracted sharks. From this came decades of dung and sudden shocks.

ACTIVE/RECOVERED ALCOHOLISM

Alcoholism: we're responsible to not drink but not for what we do under the influence see.

The active alcoholic thinks he's captain of his own ship because it's "just a beer" and it's tragic.

For the alcoholic [the allergic] the mere atom flips the switch from right to left and now he's off.

Under the influence through a mere atom the devil takes over and there's no prediction whatsoever.

Having a German mother I was born in the suds and surely imbibed flats of beer myself: kegs.

The ads with the bubbles forming on the glass was enough to trigger relapse to weeks of beer.

I called it "beer fasting"--addictive anosognosia brings on bouts of self-destruction without knowin'.

You can't predict how long it will take, how much it will cost, how many friends/family will be lost.

SOCIAL DRINKING SCAM

Alcohol is the devil for many "social drinkers" who look a little too forward to that quenching beer.

Post time got earlier and earlier and soon I drank before lunch and then at 3 a.m. in FEAR.

BRIEF OBSTACLES

I had no idea what I was like when I drank so suffered excruciatingly with failed relationships/hate.

Alcoholism is where a sweet person becomes a horrible demon in a second from a mere atom.

But when I went to A.A. I was miserable in the social hypnotic set up just like the world: yuk.

Only God in solitude--and the appreciation of the True Self found therein--cured me of this sin.

I couldn't deal with personalities and hits when curing from a terrible genetic disease like this.

I had to find a way to not need a crutch. To be self-sufficient/impervious to people in a bunch.

ALCOHOL TRIGGERS

Just when I gave it up I married an alcoholic. This sticky disease works like that and it's tragic.

Watch out: the narcissistic flip flop from idealization to devaluation triggers a female alcoholic.

He loved you as center of his world then he scorns you as a peon to be rid of: it's scary and weird.

People are officious, they want in your business. It's a major achievement: true independence.

I have friends who suicided in their sixties in fear of old age and here behold it's the highest stage!

Instead of hiding your age cuz you're over thirty why not help older people and be an example see.

Someone finally understood that my ugly anger was copying my mother when she drank sir.

BRIEF OBSTACLES

Grudges are wrong because history changes people. This is when a villain becomes an angel.

Do you know what women are like when against one they collude--yet you accept their view?

They expect you to go along with something that wasn't true until today, because they say.

-

You get so much more outa computers if you're not social. That's a block to all you can know.

HEALTH *NUT*

Breakfast: ice cream/shortbread then leaves for lunch. This fixes things and I can stay a tiny elf.

If on the right diet the skin won't reflect your age. If not it can instantly shrivel like a prune ok.

I get superior vitamineral intake thru fruits and veggie gummies and powders as a faster.

WORLD FAME

You can non-arrogantly count on being world famous if what you've done is truly tremendous.

A true theoretician on the order of Jung/Freud but with artistic significance, that's the best.

Fact: the brain declines after fifty. You can't remember anything/that's just the beginning.

I find regular writing boring/I hate it. They talk around a subject rather than just saying it.

MAKE HIM LISTEN

WE GO OUT ALONE

Stop thinking about people for you go out alone. Think only of God, now you feel loved/at home.

Life is a pie so you don't have time to say YES to everything, aye. You must vet and prioritize.

The fact you were a bad boy/mean girl may even make you more interesting now you're whole.

Having to adapt to the dumb they massacred me but it wrote.120 books on social psychology.

With repentance God whitewashes memory too. If it weren't so we'd die of embarrassment/you?

You don't do that anymore so it's a lie what they're saying. Get that straight: God is forgiving.

Asking for God's forgiveness every day is one way of softening bad feelings towards others ok.

SELF-RELIANCE IS A MUST

Self-reliance is a must, assistance is a bonus. You've gotta make plans based on just you sis.

God has put within you everything you need to manifest and actualize His vision for you see.

MAKE HIM LISTEN

That's all within you so if God brings a good helper that's a bonus and don't rely on it ever.

Women bond faster/deeper with men they're attracted to and thus it's hard to get over them too.

Since Eve was created to help Adam her first direction is relational and the bonding is all she knows.

While it may take a man 24 months to fall deepest in love it often takes a woman less than one.

A man simply does not get emotionally attached and bonded as quickly as a woman does: fact.

Adam's first edict is to work, Eve's is to help man first and this becomes obsession: a curse.

WOMEN BOND DEEPER/QUICKER

A woman bonds on a deeper level and hurts more deeply when it's broken to the point of ruin.

As Adam was made from dirt Even was pulled out of Adam and thus has a far deeper connection.

When a woman's soul is broken she develops a twisted attachment even to worthless men.

Women bond harder and faster so develop twisted attachments to clowns they call master.

Women assume "this is the one" so hurt on a far deeper level when it's done: heartbreak bond.

Men move on and they move on fast. But she's still hanging on as if he's surely coming back.

"You will want to please husband but he will lord it over you". If he leaves her heart breaks in two.

MEMORY IS THE EVIL GLUE

MAKE HIM LISTEN

What is done in relationship to keep her soul tied in perpetuity? The most important is memory.

She can't release this and move forward due to the memories, they're a glue despite treachery.

The toxic nostalgia is unrelenting. He's been gone for months/years but she's only remembering.

A broken heart can only focus on the good history while forgetting or ignoring the ugly parts/misery.

BROKEN HEART = FRAGMENTED MEMORY

A broken heart fragments memories. She remembers his lovemaking or the great vacations see.

She forgets about the beatings, brawlings and infidelities. That's shoved under the rug see.

When a woman wants a relationship to work she has a natural tendency to hold on to memories.

It's a survival issue to feed her ideal narrative lest her depression wreck the home environment.

The toxic nostalgia generates a perverted sense of love. It's important for you to see that dove.

She'll say "oh he wasn't that bad". Get that picture with you eye swollen shut then say that.

Your friends had to sit up and talk to you all night about some of the stuff--let's call them up.

In sick relationships she falls into perversion to keep his interest up in blatant self-destruction.

MEMORY AND BONDAGE

MAKE HIM LISTEN

It's memories keeping you in bondage but they're selective ones, can't you see that hon?

Good memories are selected by broken consciousness and perverted sense of love that forgets.

Worse broken bond effects on the female mean she can't relate promiscuously and not feel.

You dream of telling him things about yourself but he's a narcissist--he doesn't care and never will.

Expecting him to be interested in what her heart says is like asking a legless man to run a race.

A BROKEN HEART GETS CROOKED

A broken heart goes crooked, perverted. She can't see straight & agrees to anything to get him back.

There's nothing sadder than a crooked broken female spirit who's hardly a queen like we'd fear it.

He who hates disguises with his lips and stores up deceit--but he apologizes and she concedes.

He speaks graciously & kindly to conceal his malice but seven abominations are in his heart sis.

Tho' his hatred is covered over with guile and deceit his malevolence is soon revealed openly see.

All he has to do is apologize cuz she wants to believe with everything in her there's only love/no lies.

APOLOGIZE FOR ALL THE LIES

His apologies are nothing more but a politician's speech while she thinks: he's changed, you'll see.

He says anything to get back into your bed, tie your soul up, keep your mind numb and will dead.

MAKE HIM LISTEN

Her being continually roped in by apologies keeps her from finding the man God has for her see.

Anatomy of a fake apology: He'll show emotional sorrow, he cries. That touches her heart, aye.

Like actors on the screen they're not heartbroken they're acting--people learn how to cry see.

He says "I'm so stupid, I keep doing the same thing, I can't understand it" and again she falls for it.

"I'M SO STUPID, I'M SO STUPID"

Now this con man has you consoling him and you feel so good enabling your own destruction.

He's been fooling around and roped you back in with a fake apology and now you love him again.

The apology is very emotional filled with wild promises and that's all it takes for the jilted Mrs.

"You're the best woman ever, I can't live without you" as he has flowers delivered to her job too.

"God made me for you and you for me" He'll say but that's impossible see cuz God loves thee.

Emotional sorrow, passionate promises and love bombing gets you open to him again sis.

He knows the key to her computer and wants back into her bed. It's a story we're all familiar with.

It's the birds and bees perverted into insanity. It's God's intentions reversed by the devil see.

SICKLY CYCLICITY

And the cycle repeats itself over and again eating up years of your life without any correction.

I'm telling you this so your youth won't be wasted on fake apologies and you shoot for good guys.

Godly sorrow leads to a change in mind and behavior not his fantastic promises, so insincere.

The sincere man will ask for forgiveness and another chance showing quiet & consistent change.

The queen consciousness says: keep your flowers, stop the love bombing, hold the fake apologies.

A good man's actions quietly and consistently prove his words and he's not trying to manipulate you girl.

WHY DO THEY PERSIST WITH THE NARCISSIST?

Of course it was your siblings/cousins who hurt you, who else were you close to? It's people!

Because they're not awake living in their present moment they will bury the truth to death.

Understand these people aren't working with a full deck. Few are smart, the bulb's dim or out.

Why do they mentally check out? Because they too are being abused with the threat of a discard.

Being in the same fam they may have a trauma bond or Stockholm Syndrome so they stick to him.

If a monkey has a [likely] trauma bond with the narcissist they LOVE him/loyalty persists.

TRAUMA BONDS EXPLAIN IT ALL

MAKE HIM LISTEN

Trauma Bonds explain enigmas of gruesome twosomes or other unlikely pairings: hot/sizzling.

Their loyalty to the leader will persist even if they're getting punished, manipulated, ditched.

They're in survival mode, shut down, disassociating, not living in present, far gone or drugged.

Already in brain fog from bad association they seek to numb more with substances, addiction.

They may be trying to self-medicate to not hear the same story of the other's abuse to date.

The monkeys abusing you have also been abused, neglected & traumatized with repressed memories.

Modern people have such fragmentary memory they can't even recall their own past history.

They may be so horrified by what they do remember they keep pushing it down with whatever.

SCARED AND SLANDERED SPEECHLESS

I couldn't get up again, to defend myself. They had driven me down until I was speechless.

If you're the scapegoat or black sheep of the family they aim to punish you and punish you harshly.

So what's their motive? Vengeance, wanna get even: bitter, hateful and spiteful, that's all.

Colluding, hating, accusing: WHY? It's the spirit of jealousy pervasive in any system of lies.

If self-aware you're not a narcissist. So honey even tho' I write about it don't worry about this.

MAKE HIM LISTEN

As long as you're yoked they can talk about you like that, treat you like that, shun you like a rat.

FLYING MONKEYS IN ASSIST

Wherever there are manipulative narcissists there are multitudes of flying monkeys to assist.

Why do the flying monkeys cover up abuse? Why are they so accommodating to the narcissist?

Since monkeys are themselves abused, why do they sign up for mobbing anonymous targets too?

They are people-pleasers: followers, not leaders. Suckups to anyone appearing as conquerers.

Leader is always either a narcissist, a sociopath or a very unhealthy person. Add monkeys = bedlam.

Leader is an aggressive, domineering control freak. The flying monkeys truckle when she speaks.

I had two older sisters in collusion with a narcissist mother against me: I know all about female treachery.

In the mix there's a scapegoat, a golden child, the forgotten child and the leader of the pack.

There's always the leader of the flying monkey pack, usually a narcissist, to control dissidents.

FLYING MONKEYS ARE CODEPENDENT

Flying monkeys are very codependent with the narcissist and that's why they backstab assist.

Monkeys are in denial about everything happening to you, whether a minute ago or a year or two.

MAKE HIM LISTEN

This all goes hand in hand with the crazy three ring circus of mind games and false claims.

The monkeys veil abuse cuz they're so weak. They don't have the strength to boldly speak.

Butt heads with self-assertion and healthy boundaries? No, cowards can't confront the narcissist.

Insecure people with low self-esteem and no confidence will not confront the narcissists.

They're stinking weaklings but get em together and think about the mobbing mentality see.

I always knew they were talking about me behind the scenes. Whisperings then hush, silence see.

They're either chattering in the sanctuary or whispering behind someone's back as they walk by.

Their individual weakness is WHY they're mean as a group and WHY we have PTSD for life too.

SCAPEGOATS ARE EXPOSED TARGETS

In this predicament scapegoats feel no one listens to us and we're on our own, exposed targets.

Example: A group of 50 flying monkeys are now supermen impervious to the pain they're causing.

In the meantime they don't care if they hurt you because they have no respect for you too.

What a scary proposition, like being in a war. If you're the black sheep they just don't CARE.

First they're nice then a purge and the new ones hate you, what would you do? Re-adapt or die blue.

MAKE HIM LISTEN

The empath scapegoat can't believe the mean tyranny from family and that adds to his debility.

EXTREME MANIPULATION: SECRETS

They're manipulative, which means SECRETIVE. Evil, spiteful, vindictive to the core/pissed.

Flying monkeys are liars, divulgers of secrets and blame-shifters so the system blew up past years.

System blows up AFTER scapegoat breaks free due to lack of narcissistic supply from treachery.

A heartbreaking traumatic abusive system repeating itself intergenerationally ad nauseam.

Monkeys don't confront the abuse cuz they don't live in the present reality but pure fantasy.

They're so unhappy and unhealthy they're not in a sound mind. Divorced from reality/insane.

Actors not important, they're just caught in the web. Sensitivities determine who is selected.

Women who slept with the enemy mighta been scared to death just as they were before see.

She's used to psychopaths, sociopaths and narcissists so what's the dam difference for instance.

When the Big Act went away and he got his sons as flying monkeys life was hell and treachery.

STOP HANKERING OVER PEOPLE

Stop hankering over people. They're just a ball of mud gonna rot in the ground--love God not evil.

MAKE HIM LISTEN

Hankering over people shows a hole was stopped up. Mommy screwed up so you want Elmer Fudd.

Narcissists can display empathy but really have none, you'll eventually see it's still "all about me".

Relax, you'll be an instant hit, whatcha call a "blank entry". Where's she been all this time? Preparing.

HERO'S PATH LOOKS LIKE INSANITY

The path to the hero often looks like insanity. He's born with high energy but scattered it's troubling.

A really smart person can get so screwy it isn't funny. More intervening variables = more loony.

It's called moving on with calm firmness. No more wavering, mixture or caving into their s**t.

Narcissist Fatigue is the exhaustion coming from having normal expectations of abnormal lemons.

People tell me I should just forget it but how can I do that if it's on my mind every single minute?

"I don't need to know you, you need to know me" says the narcissist, thus he has no empathy--no need.

Narc thought: If I interrupt/push my agenda on you it's for a good cause for then you can be as good as me.

He feigned interest to get into the door but in truth his only interest is himself, he'll never ask more.

I had such weak boundaries I let people in but then the trauma that followed taught me the vital lesson.

JEZEBELS GET THEIR HIT MEN AGAINST YOU

MAKE HIM LISTEN

"Assertive" means I stand up for me, not that I change someone's mind or even make him understand.

If you can't forget that cad who hurt you so much it's cuza an early trauma glitch--that can be a bitch.

The victims of narcissists are always sympathetic empaths and he knows this, so piteous.

When women gossip as a weapon they get others as their hit men to do their dirty work from envyin'

A Jezebel like that will get "her men" against you to kill you pets or anything else to get back.

It's Jezebel's flying monkeys when everyone she knows hates you and you're miffed/confused.

They use their "male friends" as sidekicks providing muscle for whatever's got them ticked.

Stop worshipping people. They're all sinners and Jesus said even He wasn't good--only God the Father.

Never get involved with a Jezebel cuz it's not just her you're fighting but all her monkeys flying.

IN CLARITY THE PAST IS SCARY

In clarity we realize how dangerous the past was, and the only reason we're ok is cuz God saved us.

I see now every close call. A drowning man calls for God and it had to be Him Who blocked my fall.

One lucky victim got so used to being ignored as irrelevant or an extension she lost interest.

Any lady wants true intimacy: a man who's truly interested in me not as supply but sweet.

MAKE HIM LISTEN

One human law holds true: When she's done with the narcissist she's so relieved/no more blue.

She learned to never talk of herself cuz he wouldn't hear her anyway, that's how he was every day.

EXHAUSTED BY IRRELEVANCE

She became exhausted in the fog of her irrelevance to such a giant as him, his own legend.

He's in love with his own reflection but the problem is it goes awry often in the darkness of narcissism.

To maintain relationship to a narcissist your own identity must fade as you get used to being degraded.

I've never seen the speed with which a handsome man becomes an ugly man, subhuman looking.

A lack of self-control with conflict is quite evident. As the litmus test of maturity be sure to note it.

The predominance of narcissism since WWII is not true Americana which always called out selfishness.

SHORT ATTENTION SPAN

He has the attention span of a kitten as he loves you now but is entranced with another in a minute, wow.

I don't know how I ever got caught up but knowing the characteristics as here laid out saved my butt.

He didn't care what I had to say, it was all how I could enhance or serve him-- not a good husband.

A wife should never talk to another man and avoid all gaze fixation--a powerful force curbed by tradition.

MAKE HIM LISTEN

She only answers questions or talks in poetry to a man other than her husband/not be so brazen.

It's not your responsibility to prop up the narcissist. Stop being his supply, make him do it all himself.

EGO BUCKET FULL OF HOLES

I'm not gonna fill your ego bucket that's filled with leaky holes--you're gonna have to get other supply.

It's either gaze fixation or gaze aversion. Jezebel will lock on with her charms but the lady looks away.

That's the way it works, the birds and the bees to keep the race proliferating. Needs BOUNDARIES.

A wife shalt not talk to another man. That's an edict from 1881 and these are the best from early on.

Ancients knew the power of sex so put rigid boundaries on it. That's smart but moderns forget it.

I learned I had to get appreciation, acceptance and love from God only and you'll have to also.

If you don't talk to another man you won't get hurt. Stick to loved ones not people treating you like dirt.

Asking me my age, trying to make me feel over the hill. When I talk to you I wanna say "Go to hell".

Moderns have made sex so mundane it's lost it's magic but underestimating it's power can be tragic.

There's way too many opportunities for affairs. Office romances have wildly proliferated I declare.

One glance and he's all you think about for months or years. It's so powerful we must take charge!

MAKE HIM LISTEN

I was amazed when I learned it's all about sex! I couldn't believe that's all they think about, hexed.

MY GENERATION HAD WORK HABITS

My generation had work habits, projects, hobbies requiring learning. Nowadays it's all sexting.

Sex is so powerful an instinct it MUST be sublimated: channelled into something productive.

Freud saw the power of sex so the naive called him an addict but that' wasn't it--it's just reality kid.

A sex addict is a dark space. It's endless and no mature person would want involvement, nay/go away.

Tho' talking of the narcissist's lack of empathy is relieving even that is a high price to pay: fatigue.

If you couldn't get any dirt or info on the guy it could be he's not squeaky clean but just EMPTY.

For the narcissists are EMPTY: They become whatever effects THEM, they're totally ingrown sweetie.

Lessons from degradation and humiliation made us ladies and gentlemen but now how do we forget em?

Just as bad is Mental Adultery. You should never do that because fantasy becomes reality.

What woman hasn't been degraded by a dam man? Well now men are degraded by women the same.

DYSFUNCTION MAKES US HOMESICK: IRONY

I feel like I'm in sixth grade on my way to summer camp. Except I spent it all in the infirmary, homesick.

MAKE HIM LISTEN

Children from dysfunction get the most homesick when away from it but those loved can multi-adapt.

For the first time I'm in a loving, secure home cuz I own it, I control it and no one I don't like gets in it.

A life of porous boundaries in the children of dysfunction is one big hog pen of bedlam as evil flows in.

If people know you've a broken marriage they'll come against you quick cuz it's a downed hedge.

The major tool the narcissist uses to make you feel crazy is getting your friends/esp family against you.

The narcissist always portrays as good guy so later with her outbursts he can play the victim, a lie.

DID THE CHURCH HELP?

HELL NO. The modern church is pure social hall religion and I hated it more than sick society itself.

I want the TRUTH about heaven and hell, sin and repentance. I want the holy rollers again.

I interned at V.A. and learned all about people there. Not the patients, it's the staff who's insane I declare.

WHAT IS ATTACHMENT INJURY?

With attachment injury you hold on to impossible situations or recreate them with surrogates.

Attachment injuries are a turning away in the form of abandonment, emotional neglect or betrayal.

Attachment injuries occur with dismissal or disregard to the emotional well being of the other.

MAKE HIM LISTEN

Injuries feel like being unseen, unheard, unknown, not affirmed, not welcomed and ignored.

The injuries can be covert and subtle but cumulative as the nervous system picks up on it.

Attachment injuries aren't about presence but absence and thus frightening in emptiness.

Empty interactions can re-code the brain, it's maps and all its nervous system responses.

Trauma occurs in those times you were reaching for support and connection but came up empty.

Tho' the culprit of the injury is unaware OR if the event is minor it may be a MAJOR TRAUMA.

If disconnected or ignored the result is SHAME for things from self-hate to fearing the landlord.

I grew up with a sense of SHAME over everything, based on disconnection to the family.

It hurt so much in the solar plexus: a pain in the gut like a horse kicked me and later an eating rut.

It's Jezebel's flying monkeys when everyone she knows hates you and you're miffed/confused.

SHAME IS THE RESULT OF DISCONNECTION

Emotionally connected members don't have shame as events are not so hotly remembered.

You NEEDED emotional connection in that moment and didn't get it and the result was PANIC.

Picking emotionally unavailable partners then relentlessly pursuing them like they mattered.

MAKE HIM LISTEN

The deadhead triggers the earliest trauma when the same thing or worse happened with momma.

The core beliefs (I don't matter) perpetuate the old patterns of relating (try to change him or her).

Emotional attunement with others is nourishment, being fed or we have early trauma instead.

Attunement is an unconscious social synchrony that guides empathy and then good report.

Healing means strengthening, honing and maturing our neurological and FELT senses.

EXISTENTIAL PANIC

Existential Panic is how I'd describe it, a terror in the gut's solar plexus about the environment.

A HOSTILE environment: I picked up on it instantaneously and hated every moment of it.

They were liberals or lukewarm Christians and they hated how I thought about all things.

I picked up on their evil thoughts and projections and just wanted to get away from ALL of them.

Who creates all this trouble? People. PEOPLE = TROUBLE so can we live in a bubble?

THE MORE INTRICATE THE PATTERNS

The more intricate the patterns the more VIOLENT the system reaction with "shifts" in them.

MAKE HIM LISTEN: Women not acting thru intuition but force-feeding narrative how they're victims.

MAKE HIM LISTEN

When things aren't working we wanna crack the code to get it going but only create division.

What you're saying is the problem is HIM cuz he's not relating but that just pushes him away.

Choose a Christian who loves you cuz he's supposed to not wavering with flighty feelings.

And NEVER let an EX jump over for a quickie: If it's off, it's off--don't degrade yourself honey.

ESCAPE INTO THE RIGHT BRAIN

When there's been a switch there's nothing you can say to bring it back but only make it worse.

NOW'S the time to go into the right brain, get high, look to eternity, tell God your Father Hi.

Demanding more of the other's attention sets up more of the same and that is the game.

By becoming hyperalert to the partner YOU become less available, caught up in a soap opera.

Caught up like this you're limiting your ability to be present and thus a lot less magnetic.

Don't limit your ability to be available to the other by being hyperalert to his sins or whatever.

We all want emotional closeness but it's how to get it that's misunderstood for you can't demand it.

Failing to figure out how they're failing you and being compelled to act like a dam sleuth.

All because the brain works on PATTERNS and the loss of pattern recognition is ADDICTION.

MAKE HIM LISTEN

While you're holding back emotionally you're also being avoided--healthy relating is challenging.

AT HOME I'M FREE

The world is too dirty for me when there's not even a semblance of decency but at home I'm free.

Break the pattern by not focusing on the other person and questioning the relation.

To prevent this from happening we need to do the honest work of prescreening our associates.

If they do not value the level of emotional connection that we do I doubt it can be overridden.

We need to have common ground then grow together, not some therapy to relate better.

Relationship thrills are NOT from panic, urgency, fear or nervously learning new relating skills.

System inversions: preoccupied and anxious attachment brings hyper-distance in reaction.

YOU are unavailable when sucked into your preoccupied thinking, whether of sin or him.

Systems theory: all mental illness is rooted in attachment trauma--we are "framed" by it.

The STILL FACE experiments: no eye contact, no reaction, no love = mental illness.

People are waking up so fast cuza this Epstein thing. Any way it can happen it's a gladdening.

By framing us they mess us up for life or we take that suit off/put a new one on, and go on.

MAKE HIM LISTEN

We get a NEW identity: the spirit of Jesus Christ but also the unique seed symbol of our OWN.

The old man is totally gone, we are made NEW and there is no more condemnation.

As "white" and pure as snow.

LIMBIC RESONANCE OR IT'S HELL MAN

Limbic Resonance means we're meeting emotionally in a system that rolls along quite happily.

It's the emotional processing component of healing from attachment trauma that matters.

Systems Theory and Attachment Injury is talking about the same realm truthfully.

Why did the worst sinners become the best saints? Cuz they were the MOST happy to escape.

Ok so he's a prosperity teacher with a Christian background--not what you want, so what.

Never let em assume a sale by recapping you in a different view: Learn how to argue!

With attachment injury you hold on to impossible situations or recreate them with surrogates.

LIBERAL SISTERS CAME BACK TO ABUSE US

There were decades of silent agreement to the liberal view or they'd get violent too.

Sisters went to liberal colleges and came back to abuse us all for not going along with it.

Suddenly my old mother had to hear about gays, abortion, anti-family/Christianity/the west.

MAKE HIM LISTEN

Mom's world was turned upside down by this communist crap largely Cultural Marxism.

My world was shattered when accused of "white privilege" at 15 because I drove a Mustang.

It was a bunch of shovedowns from the left but we didn't have the TOOLS to object...

And so we drank. If you can't make sense of the world just create your own inner world.

Sister married a Hindu and our Christian heritage was lost as mom drank/sang "we're ALL ONE".

We're not all one, we all like being with our own kind and that's perfectly natural for ALL humans.

Geographical relocation gives you a chance to leave it all behind--cut evil memory, become refined.

ONCE IN SAFETY EXPECT PTSD

Once in safety I experienced PTSD as memories unpeeled like an onion of California demons.

Having splashed into the desert with attachment injury I proceeded to REPEAT it in tragedies.

Once the hero slips and then HANGS ONTO lower characters his demise his soon and sudden.

That ACCOUNTS for his spiraling down: his hanging on to lower characters and comforting sins.

Recap. We can sense emotional distancing and dogs will bark when they sense it in a family.

Our SINS bring emotional distancing and if there is no repenting, blaming = more descending.

MAKE HIM LISTEN

Caught in attachment injury of the earliest and most primal kind, I was a walking robot and blind.

All have sins and I fell into my bag, unknowingly and as if it were perfectly natural to be that way.

In California I swam in muddy waters and tried my whole life to get completely clean from it.

The liberal incursion into a Christian family took me three decades to figure out, thus 100 books.

The liberal incursion into our family was like a BIG BLACK CLOUD that ruined life/kept us down.

We must either heal family relationships or FREE OURSELVES from them/existential panic.

SEE it, then grieve it: both what happened in the family and what didn't happen, now move up.

ATTACHMENT TRAUMA: BEING IGNORED

INJURY: An experience impacting your attachment system from which you have not recovered.

This is an unintegrated attachment injury: being unseen, unheard, misunderstood, unknown.

When this happens over a period of time the main symptom is INTRUSION in body, emotions, mind.

When we can't make peace with the trauma it distorts reality/creates longing for a partner.

When it ends we get activated with these intrusive thoughts and feelings: obsessiveness.

With obsessive trauma/injury the minds starts looping about him or her and it's torture.

MAKE HIM LISTEN

Attachment trauma creates longing--distorting reality as mind's hijacked thru intrusive thoughts.

The desire to connect is to feel some sense of safety and reassurance, so it really gets to us.

Always looping about em: The intrusive, deceptive, ongoing assault of relentless thinking.

If you were in deep sin it's no mystery the lowness you attracted in, so just forgive em.

INTRUSIVE THINKING STARTS WITH BETRAYAL

It starts with betrayal then the trauma lowers our life level then bad attractions take us to hell.

Over time this wears us down and we're confused, so it's just home, pets, rockingchair and the news.

When I think of them it's rejection then shame. If I'm rid of them it's new arenas and fame.

The mind loops in cycles: "What about this, remember that one time, I should call..."

Repeatedly bombarded with memories, events, images, beliefs about world and the self.

What happened, what didn't happen, what should have happened = nature of intrusive thinking.

Feeling a need to connect to that person, for safety and validation, it becomes urgent, oh man.

Stuck in unresolved attachment trauma I was like this until to Jesus I shifted emotional dependence.

Intrusive thinking would make sense since attachment injuries are survival related.

MAKE HIM LISTEN

There's an intensity that comes with unresolved trauma: "Is everything ok, is everything ok?"

The profound desire to come back together or be with that person is survival-related/primal.

The problem with intrusive thinking is we get so caught up in em we start to believe them.

PRESENT LONGING MIRRORS THE BEGINNING

The intensity of the longing is taken as proof that we need to salvage the relationship, hah.

No reconciliation can begin with intrusive thinking (fear of loss) since you're at your lowest.

Most often the attachment injury comes from childhood.

Mostly the attachment injury comes from childhood or as adults, betrayal or abandonment.

Early relationships with family create a template for how we re-create adult relationships.

Present longing for the adult partner MIRRORS the degree to which I was unseen/unheard.

INJURY: The degree to which I was misunderstood--NOT KNOWN--in my own family.

BETRAYAL IS ATTACHMENT INJURY

Triggered attachment injury like betrayal = intrusive thinking which shows up as longing.

Longing for the other person, the "object" of our desire to reconnect/stop the trauma again.

The degree of longing for the other MIRRORS the degree to which we were early ignored.

MAKE HIM LISTEN

The unresolved hurt and grief at being ignored and neglected is projected onto CURRENT loss.

The intensity of the feelings IS the childhood grief surging out after being unresolved.

They can't imagine how much you've change so they can ONLY think: you were always that way.

Keep saying: These painful thoughts are from being system-disconnected resulting in shame.

The SKILL needed is to separate out the object longed for with the intensity of the emotion.

When we get worn down by it we send messages to get em back but it's still not right for us.

An attachment injury when you weren't seen, heard, known nor understood in your family system.

Wanting someone from the past is like going into a graveyard. Face it/mourn it/reject it, it's over.

I don't matter, disconnection = SHAME = addictions as coping devices = SHAME/I don't matter

RELEASING VICTIMHOOD FOR SUCCESS

You must say goodbye to your abandoned self and carrying that as your identity around.

To get access to resource (come up the ladder) we must release the wounded identity more.

The abandoned one isn't who I am anymore and I'm willing to say goodbye: now you're there.

When you see it there's a grieving period--do it. Now put on your real, TRUE identity: work it.

MAKE HIM LISTEN

Instead of seeing it as abandonment I simply see it as the way SIN and human systems work.

If your parent did not LIKE you it's another form of attachment trauma and symptoms accrue.

It's so frightening the child can't even say "My parent doesn't like me" but we say it in therapy.

It's highly unpleasant to let in the crushing truth and reality that your parent didn't like you.

NORMALIZE IT TO DISTANCE IT

In saying that we NORMALIZE it then are able to DISTANCE from it so symptoms disperse.

Before doing this we may feel just plain odd, unwanted, purposeless and an embarrassment.

When you're 5 or even 32 it's nearly impossible to admit your parent dislikes you.

If mom or dad doesn't like me I feel insecure, I can't make decisions and it brings confusion.

Grieving is resignation: it's a dropping into or settling into--making peace with the truth.

And that's how we discover some freedom and lightness, making peace with the past.

It impacts your feeling of worth and feelings of insecurity as well as relationships today.

Yes, the mere [painful] recognition that your parent didn't like you opens you to new resources.

Early loss of parents can make one independent and self-referencing or shut them down completely.

MAKE HIM LISTEN

Shut down: Feeling imploded and not fully able to move into their next chapter of life.

Grief and major life upheavals can get in the way or act as a catalyst and open you up, ok?

MOVED TO A GHOST TOWN TO BE RID OF EM

When I got restraining orders against all those boys my life changed in the twinkling of an eye.

They couldn't stand my mental independence and sought to run me out of a small desert town.

So I moved out to a ghost town just to be rid of em and it became my castle and home.

I don't like women any better cuz I had two sisters and a mother and they didn't like me either.

As long as you're a victim that means one-down: the opposite to fully self-determinant.

So we gotta let the victim identity go to stop those thoughts below and really start to grow.

How about being an inventor, an entrepreneur, a discoverer, a pathbreaker, a homemaker.

ATTACHMENT INJURY = TRAUMA ENERGY

Attachment injuries encode as **TRAUMA ENERGY** determining our perceptions/responses.

Sometimes over-closeness is unsettling, revealing vulnerabilities and we want OUT RIGHT NOW.

But overdistance brings instant panic leaking from the original attachment trauma injury.

MAKE HIM LISTEN

Trauma is coded into the body at the level of activation by vulnerability and intimacy.

Most vulnerable and intimate in relationships = most apt to activate original trauma.

Trauma energy is described as "looping" as it has that repetitive quality--how boring.

Level of activation: if the original trauma was a "9" in intensity it links with deeper relationships.

The "9" activation won't be showing in more shallow friendships with intimacy level of 1-8.

MAPS THE BRAIN AND IMPACTS NERVOUS SYSTEM

It's covert developmental emotional trauma thru time mapping brain/impacting nervous system.

The absurd and ridiculous things I said and did, as if possessed by another being and outa control.

As I look back it's surrealistic. Words and actions as uprushes from the unconscious--"autonomisms".

It wasn't "me" that was activated but a deep, primal archetype from the collective unconscious.

Some really weird stuff--"ego alien material" it's called, demons from the beginning of it all.

You gotta be clear, whole and in control to reject this stuff. If dense or weak they take over/it's rough.

FORGET SPECIFICS AND SEE THE FOREST

I don't know the specifics of my attachment trauma but the results were terrible I tell ya.

MAKE HIM LISTEN

Like a car accident encoded into the nervous system at a 9.5 intensity—it's a lasting tragedy.

What if you were not able to discharge that trauma energy collected in your nervous system?

I was always scared to death of my mother and had nightmares until we became drinking buddies.

To me she seemed illogical, brutal, aggravating, always on me = there was no concentrating.

As young as five I had thoughts of killing her but that turned inward later and it was me I was after.

EMOTIONAL BLOCK

I developed intellectually but not emotionally--I had to suffer to draw lines and break free.

People will run you right over unless you draw lines and demand respect. If not, you're dead.

Well I didn't know that nor did I know I should care--I had to be run over, and over, and over.

What everyday man or woman knew I did not know--that was from the trauma, the original blow.

The brain and nervous system was on overload and couldn't make sense of the world, overwhelmed.

STORED AT LEVEL OF ACTIVATION

The trauma is stored at the level of vulnerability--at the DEPTH of that connection you see.

Why am I not freaking out at a lover but not a friend? Cuz trauma is stored at the level of activation.

MAKE HIM LISTEN

Repetition compulsion: The same drama loops through our mind until we work thru trauma.

Repetition compulsion: Of choosing mates that won't love you over and over again.

It means unmet needs from childhood and a PATTERN of people not meeting your needs.

Ironically the one we want the most usually is the one who is the worst for us and it's unconscious.

The object of desire is not that great but he's put on a pedestal cuz he poked that early snake.

Part of the repetition is old neuropathways stuck in the same pattern, we are robots man.

Just cuz time has passed doesn't mean we don't go into adulthood with the same child patterns.

FACE THE EARLY CREEPS OR DENY AND REPEAT

Face the early creeps or go into denial and repeat.

Solution: Create NEW neuropathways that are correct: being loved/extinguishing the defect.

Its the abuser that "feels right" because that attachment injury was imprinted in early life.

You were IMPRINTED towards a rejecting type of person, a real jerk is your best life's lesson.

You're not really holding on to Jack but a projection of unmet needs from childhood, a lack.

You can't get over Jack if you're idolizing him from false facts--you must see him for what he is.

MAKE HIM LISTEN

I idolized a man not cuza who he was--a boring bummer--but cuz I was "back there".

With this simple knowledge of how the brain works I pray you stop following and fawning over jerks.

Don't give em so much credit when you're projecting YOUR good qualities onto them!

The chances of them being narcissist (tho' sweet as pie) and you being codependent are HIGH.

Only by truly letting go do we realize it isn't this person, it's trauma energy from the beginning.

You must let go of what YOU THINK will solve black hole emptiness, it's how the brain works.

THE FLIP FLOP OF STORED ENERGY

He's simply the present object in the brain map but other than that, just an ordinary chap.

He just got the full wallop of the trauma energy stored for decades--the giant flip flop.

Then he's long gone for good and all you can do is blame yourself--you unlovable evil elf!

MEET that unmet need as he's walking away--meet yourself and you'll see it's just an imprint, ok?

USE PRESENT GRIEF TO ERASE TEMPLATE

We need to realize this person we're projecting onto does not care about us-- ESSENTIAL, do this.

You can't prove yourself to nor change them--that would take their personal development.

MAKE HIM LISTEN

Systems theory: mental illness is based in attachment injury and a compulsion to repetition.

Drunk feminist mother keeps her down, flip flops abound, she loves those calling her clown.

The degree to which you hurt over bad mates is how much you **NEED** to, to extinguish the game.

They may not be bad but they're bad for you and that's the point--they don't want you.

Use the present situation-surrogate for the **GRIEF** needed to erase the original template.

LIFE-CHANGING SOLUTION: Realize your parents didn't like you and neither did this dude.

SO YOUR EX HAS NEW SUPPLY

So your EX has new supply and he's moved on really quickly and nothing else makes sense.

He hasn't found the new love of his life but simply gotten new supply--other than that, apathy.

Narcissistic Supply: keep that in mind, it's not about "feelings" which you have day and night.

For those patterns don't go away because of a beautiful face or new thrills, they will **PREVAIL**.

DEVALUATION PHASE: NOW HE COMES OUT

The version of their personality that comes out in the **DEVALUATION** phase is dormant right now.

But when he's triggered he'll pull the rug out through the dirtiest tricks he can, bet on it.

MAKE HIM LISTEN

His charming manipulation devices kept his supply on the hook but now suddenly its all forsook.

And when that real person comes out, just when you're heavy in attachment injury, omg.

Their patterns are deep, their lost self/empty core, how they relate to others/they see the world.

MOVE ON AHEAD NOW—LET DEAD BURY DEAD

Of course God can change anyone but walk away cuz you're busy and need to GET ER DUN.

LET IT GO by realizing it was all a bad movie reflecting a glitch in your baby history.

The narcissistic injury in him is SO profound that the patterns will prevail, but you're free my gal.

Is this person really personality-disordered or were they right all along in saying I'm the problem?

You're alone but they're in a new relationship proving they can do it and the problem is you?

They're just acting out their pattern (for supply) and you don't ever have to again, bye bye.

Transcend the intensity of your emotion's mind to the WISE mind, made to counteract it.

THEY'RE JUST DOING THEIR THING/RUNNING THEIR NUMBER

There's the idolization and love-bonding side but then there's the devaluation and I died.

Never again to be on a wheel with that person and have your lives dictated to by narcissism.

Even from afar, RELEASE the hold that they have on you.

MAKE HIM LISTEN

Narcissist attachment style: charmingly suck you in then throw you away when beguiled.

You're in mourning and healing/he's soaring and self-adoring but his symptoms will be prevailing.

Now the nervous preoccupied orients to the loss and the dismissive avoidant pulls as boss.

The dismissive/emotionally unavailable would rather hurt than be hurt and he knows how to do it.

The dismissive can easily emotionally reject since they never really emotionally connected.

Dismissives hide their emotions so much you're blindsided when they suddenly up and leave.

De-activating strategies: With the other's pullback they start to do things to bring emotion back.

You're not going to get reassurance from a dismissive, just de-activating strategies.

Instances of Deactivating Strategies are incurring jealousy, flirtations, glances, accusations.

JEALOUSY FOR CLOSENESS OR DISTANCE

Anxious mates will incur jealousy for more closeness, dismissives do it to build walls/back away.

In other words what you should give from this is most people are a HOUSE OF DEMONS.

And their injuries so deep and profound only God himself can make em whole/heal the clowns.

The fear of being alone for life is a black tunnel perceived thru the vision of a five year old.

MAKE HIM LISTEN

Moments in our history of younger selves--when we were truly alone, abandoned and felt it.

You really truly were rejected. You really truly were IGNORED. Face it and this nightmare is over.

SUDDEN LOVE LOSS: SURVIVAL MODE

What it's like to be suddenly flooded with the absence of connection is beyond description.

Since attachment is linked to survival in the species, our whole system explodes in emergency.

Wow, watch out: "I'm really rejected here" activates this core primal SURVIVAL fear.

END: when we finally have potential to DROP INTO this stream of panic and convert it to good.

Similarly I'll never have another housekeeper around or it's just demons and archetypal intrusions.

Compassion coming thru government is NO compassion cuz it requires force. Ben Shapiro

The question is asked: does the narcissist miss me? He misses qualities of what you offered him.

If the narcissist misses you it is because he doubts his new source of supply, that's why.

Or he may be getting bored since narcissists can't handle stagnancy or consistency.

They can't handle expectations put on them consistently and thus may turn back to thee.

The dual bomb of entitlement and feeling easily bored leads to seek greener pastures.

MAKE HIM LISTEN

They like the spike of the dysfunction, the emotional outlet and the ability to abuse someone.

While his new supply starts to expect more things [has needs and wants] he craves the past.

HE DEVALUED AND DISCARDED YOU

You symbolize devaluation-and-discard, so don't you go back and instead get a NEW start.

He devalued you and put you in a psychosis of uncertainty and dread, now don't go back.

It could be they felt "seen" cuz they could abuse you and you still stuck around the fiend.

Their taste for drama and blood doesn't go away, they'll get you again some day.

They become the boss with a taste for chaos, hurting others, damaging, creating loss.

One of the biggest problems in therapy is ABUSE AMNESIA--it's tricky to remember all of it.

A song comes up and we recall only the good parts, we become swooped up to the false.

You don't miss you, your personality and traits but what you offered them, nothing to hate.

So they don't miss you and you don't miss them (the abuser) unless it's a trauma bond that's all.

Think how he made you feel: lost, abandoned, used, discarded, of no value/doesn't matter.

How could you miss that? Forget his courting phase, you were vulnerable and it was all false.

MAKE HIM LISTEN

THEY CAN TURN ON THE CHARM

Men all know what to say to females emotionally needy especially those without a daddy.

Your idea of missing and their's are greatly different. There's is supply, your's is endearment.

You're a great hostess and he misses your supply--that's not missing YOU so say goodbye.

Whether intentionally or not, that creep became a master manipulator of your worst fears.

It's the Fallen Hero Syndrome when previous fans become foes as you're goin' down.

He'll put you in a defective car, he'll make fun of you at the bar, he'll purposely take bad pictures.

SELF-LOVE STAVES OFF ABUSE

It's simple: when in an abusive relationship it means we're not loving ourselves.

I know: when family relationships were not equal nor respectful to me as a person, I fell down.

I had to build my own reality and the boundaries maintaining it before I stood up for myself.

It takes two things to stave off abuse, aggression, imposition: your own reality and boundaries.

The poor sickly continue to vote for the evil elites because they know no better, that's it.

He's charming and acts interested cuz that works to gain supply--learn about jerks or die.

MAKE HIM LISTEN

His biggest supply need is sex--never allow this. No casual drop ins, no quickies or favor-doing.

NO casual sex after an emotional disconnection. They can't have one foot out, one foot in.

For casual post-relationship sex tears open the wound of the original attachment injury.

Post-relationship sex that INSIDE you know is going nowhere, cuz he discarded you girl.

Nothing more intimate: Post-sex tears open the previous attachment injury so NEVER allow it!

NEVER ALLOW CASUAL EX-SEX

He becomes charming to get you back for sex--he wants his supply that's all, it's all effects.

The contradiction of buttering you up then discarding you [AGAIN] is a deep trauma friend.

You may even buy his charm and think you're getting back together again, then be dropped again.

Some of you may even be "sucked" in for years of this vicious and sick cycle of abuse.

Cut it loose, you're in delusion. There's a reason God hates fornication and it's not good for women.

He walked away now he has NO hold on you--no partial commitments or mind-screws.

That kinda man is a walking time bomb and will keep you on your toes but baby he's no fun.

DON'T BE A DAM FOOL

MAKE HIM LISTEN

So you didn't have a loving Dad to compare him to--shift your love to God and He'll protect you.

I wouldn't suffer anything shifty and crazymaking ever again cuz I'm my own friend.

Don't do anything to make him listen, just see the gist here then love yourself hon'.

The hungry man returns to where he last got food--don't be his SEX SUPPLY or be a FOOL!

Of course he wants you--he may even see you in a good light temporarily, that's just sexual reality.

Women who think they're getting as much out of a post-relationship quickie are DAM FOOLS.

Women must return to chastity for their own good and dignity to avoid these heartbreaks.

Do it now: commit to chastity and get a husband who is loyal and can provide and protect.

Men: avoid all sluts, you must. Not even as friends, it's a nasty spirt friend. Be faithful and loyal.

AGEISM

Let no one constrain you due to your age. Ageism is even worse than racism said the sage.

Old age opens you up to MORE it does not constrain to less but a youthist culture is a pest.

Their rude AGE comments turn a happy rainbow into a black cloud and that's AGEISM man.

You are seen by a category--your bust size, your AGE--and that is so constricting/derogatory.

MAKE HIM LISTEN

Suddenly, you're nothing. You've gone from feeling enriched to just a number, horrifyingly.

Shut up about things don't exist and concentrate on what does exist before you're hit.

FOOD MEANS MOTHER AND AGE SHOULDN'T MATTER

Food addiction is more primal than sex addiction, it's deeper/earlier and food means mother.

It's not that you can't face your age, but that they would say it, using it as a wedge.

Well we all have to go thru it so good luck to ya. You'll see it's worse than racism soon.

We're a married couple--both saints--protecting each others's total solitude, how cool.

We want to write our own day not always be in reaction to another interruption.

If my dog can sense sudden emotional distance, a person many times more if apprehensive.

So keep your mouth shut about age or anything else that objectifies you as if you don't exist.

They use subtle conservational tricks to bully you into looking dumb. Frustrating, huh?

The general pattern: "So you're saying..." then they oversimplify and make you look lame.

GOVERNMENT THOUGHTS

A small **LIBERAL** desert town. Here they put little bombs in the PO boxes of Republicans.

Free markets bring prosperity--they're inherently moral but AOC calls em "irredeemable".

MAKE HIM LISTEN

No government can make sure the outcome is equal just that the rules are evenly applied.

You can't compel people to wanna hang out with you but that's what they're trying to do.

Once the government starts to compel association it gets ugly cuz who operates as the gun?

Telling us who we MUST live next to, compelling association--it's a loose cannon/no fun.

Forced integration is hell on earth--to be suddenly surrounded by strangers is like God's wrath.

People facilitating your ability to major in gender studies is a form of education compulsion.

FATARIAN THOUGHTS BACK THEN

No More Heartburn Smoothie: Lotsa strawberries, 1/2 cucumber, 2 celery, tab coconut cream

Follow with couple spoons of nutbutter and that's enough for the day, you'll see.

Tuna-fish salad: fine-dice celery, cucumber, white onion and black olives. Mash in can albacore, lemon juice and salt to taste.

When it comes to food it's not a matter of what's good but what doesn't hurt and is fresh, succulent, delicious.

COMPLETION INTO SUCCESS AT LAST

You're finally done. Now just get high and wait to be discovered. Karen Kellock.

What you've done is what NO one else has ever done nor even tried so hold your head high!

MAKE HIM LISTEN

They were silent years but not lost years. It was underground anarchy: debunk/reconstruct.

I had to be totally alone in the desert wilderness to see all this. Solitude = bliss, intelligence.

How beautiful the sky is for the first time in decades since Trump removed the chemtrails.

RECAP: My nervous system picked up our disconnect and since we're "family" it made me a wreck.

Just cuz you say you're done or complete doesn't mean it is--it's over when God says it kid.

God uses the weak and foolish things like me to surprise the wise and what a high!

ONE WORD from God changed my life forever. I was over the other, visited by the Father.

I lived to please God not man but in obeying Him I serve my man cuz that's God's plan.

Satan sets us up to get us upset. It's always a test and growth's about overcoming the pests.

LEFT WING INSTITUTIONS ARE COLLAPSING

As liberal colleges are dying, conservative Christian colleges are exploding and surging.

More and more liberal left-wing institutions are collapsing--they're falling apart ya see.

Liberal institutions are imploding under the weight of their own absurdity having the power.

Elitist institutions speak a language we can't understand or find odious--so it's over, adios.

MAKE HIM LISTEN

Being without puts you at the mercy of others or slaves to a dying system. Prepare man.

It's OK for the non-whites to resist replacement but when whites resist they're RACISTS?

THINKERS NEED TWO HOUSES

A married couple of TWO thinkers/creators/writers must live in two houses a courtyard apart.

The intricacies of human social nature is such that the CONFUSION is just too too much.

I have it better than all other women: I get all benefits but don't have to live with him.

Not that I don't love him but have been thru the ringer with humans and just wanna be alone.

An older female writer, that's what this is—has had it, is exhausted when she's finally made it.

Women wore strapless in the fifties, a moral generation but it's immodest now, in the most immoral?

It isn't the fact that they said you were old but that they would use that as a tactic—it's a cruel attack.

Men and women are different but I'm different too you know. Accept my buzzcut/I'll accept your beard.

MAKE HIM LISTEN

Nothing's as productive as musing/looking out the window. These are creative times: fertile.

It's wrong to have ten, twenty, a hundred cats but it's ok to have five and love them for life.

KK BOOKS: DIFFERENT IS DANGEROUS

Karen Kellock Books: Social Psych Theory $6 plus. Hix Politix and the KK Picturestrips $5 bucks.

A discovery triggers subconscious analogies in THEM--it does not TELL them what to think instead.

Most important step for all tasks: Assembling your materials then the project completes itself.

Each quip is a brutal reversal and resolution to the contradiction all in one, it's relieving/fun.

ALL ASPECTS OF THE NEW SOCIAL PSYCH

I've hereby explained all aspects of the new Social Psychology. I hope it helps, goodbye.

I'm going to resolve to be decisive even when there is pushback, in fact that's the test: pass it.

I was able to do it my way. That is to write what I think then without an audience attract that ONE link.

It's based on a lifetime of work, not blowing my own horn. There's a big difference and I see it all around.

They attacked you for being different—it was dangerous--but that's what fills your bank accounts.

Stop having remorse cuz with death like a vapor it'll all disperse: no memory after the hearse.

MAKE HIM LISTEN

You die = all those things you're thinking, planning and fearing have no more bearing for eternity.

Friend says: I saw you as a spirit getting caught up in things but always returning quickly.

She wants to make him listen and he wants to escape to his tool room. I know, I've argued with em.

That nuisance Jezebel wants you to think she's won but stick around you'll see her go down AGAIN.

Biblically the enemy flourishes like the olive tree but then is cut down like dead grass—it's a promise sweetie.

I'm gonna die and can't waste time so please stay away, just as I begged you to my whole life ok.

People are creepy and they come and go. Stick to neighbors you know, avoid demons below.

She's young enough to be my granddaughter and yet she's jealous of me, is this not insanity?

If you can't allow housekeepers in cuz they steal everything, are these not the last days ya' think?

100 KAREN KELLOCK BOOKS

AFFINITY OR MISERY
AGELESS CORNUCOPIA
AMERICA AWAKE!
AMERICA'S DAFT ERA
ARTS OF PALEO FASTING
AUTOPHAGY ON CHEATERS
BACKSTABBING NEUROTICS
BETRAYAL TRAUMA
BOOMERS AND BROKENNESS
BOOT ON NECK
CHAMPION GUIDES
COMMIE NUTHOUSE
COMMIES
COMMUNIST SPIRIT
CONTAGION OF MADNESS
CONTAGIOUS MADNESS
CULTURE CLASH BASHED
DAFT LEFT
DAILY FASTARIAN
DAM RATS
DIVERSITY IS CRUELTY
E-RACE WHITE
EVIL FREAKS (Beyond Gross)
THE END OR A BEND?
FEMALE BULLIES AND FEMI-NAZIS
FEMALE CARNALITY
FEMALE DUMB DOWN
FEMALE POWER DRIVE
FEMINISM AND RUIN 1 & 2
FIX FOR MISFITS
FOOLS & TRAMPS
FREEDOM SPEAKING
FRENEMY ENABLER
FRENEMY LIAR
FRENEMY THIEF
FRENEMY TRAITOR
TRENEMY TYRANT
GENIUS IS HELD DOWN
GLOBALISLAM
GOD USES THE FLAWED
HAZE OF THE LATTER DAYS

KAREN KELLOCK PH.D.

M.S. Political Science, San Diego State. Ph.D. in Psychology, University of California Irvine. Postdoctoral: UCI School of Medicine, Dept. of Psychiatry [NIMH Grants]. Developed the Debris Theory of Disease, a theory of system pathology in 120 books and 22 textbooks for the general public. The theory has a general formula: All disease is obstruction, all recovery is elimination, all success is attraction. The three obstructions are people, habit and food. Remove obstruction and snap to your goals, waiting in the wings.